W9-CMS-596

LLAMAS AND ALPACAS

BY ELLIS M. REED

The Child's World®
childsworld.com

Published by The Child's World®
1980 Lookout Drive • Mankato, MN 56003-1705
800-599-READ • www.childsworld.com

Photographs ©: Shutterstock Images, cover (llama),
cover (alpaca), 2, 3, 6, 10, 13, 15, 20, 21, 24
(llama), 24 (alpaca); Colleen Johansen/Shutterstock
Images, 5; Lisa Stelzel/Shutterstock Images, 9; Irina
Mos/Shutterstock Images, 11; iStockphoto, 14, 17;
Juni Samos/Shutterstock Images, 19

Copyright © 2020 by The Child's World®
All rights reserved. No part of this book may be
reproduced or utilized in any form or by any means
without written permission from the publisher.

ISBN 9781503835931
LCCN 2019943064

Printed in the United States of America

ABOUT THE AUTHOR

Ellis M. Reed writes and edits
children's books. During the
winter, she wears thick socks
made from alpaca wool.

TABLE OF CONTENTS

Wooly Body

A **mammal** runs up to a fence. It sticks out its long neck. It has **wool** on its body. It has two soft toes on each foot. The rest of its **herd** runs up to join it. Are they llamas or alpacas? How are they different?

Most llamas live on farms.

Llamas like living in groups.

2

Llamas

Llamas have long heads and long ears. Their ears are shaped like bananas. Llamas can weigh up to 250 pounds (110 kg). Llamas live in herds. They do not live in the wild.

Llamas have thick wool. It is coarse. It is white, black, or brown. People use llama wool to make rugs, rope, and jackets.

Many llamas live in the mountains of South America. They do not need a lot of water. They can eat many different plants.

Some famers put tassels on their llamas' ears to tell their llamas apart from other farmers' llamas.

Most llamas are gentle. But they sometimes attack **predators**. Llamas may hiss or spit at them. Some llamas guard other **livestock**.

Some llamas can walk more than 15 miles (24 km) a day while carrying packs.

Some people use llamas as pack animals. These llamas carry goods on their backs. They can walk for a long time before getting tired. The packs can be heavy. If a pack is too heavy, the llama may stop walking.

Alpacas

Alpacas have short noses and small heads. Their ears are pointy. Alpacas can weigh up to 200 pounds (90 kg).

Alpacas do not live in the wild. People raise them in herds to keep the animals safe.

Alpacas are originally from South America, but they are now raised all over the world.

Alpacas have to be sheared, or have their wool cut, about once a year when their wool gets too thick.

14

People raise alpacas for their soft wool. It is very light and strong. People use it for sleeping bags, coats, and warm clothes. There are 22 different colors of alpaca wool.

Most alpacas are gentle and shy. They can be trained with simple commands. They can be trained to live in barns.

Alpacas eat grass and hay. They run away when they are scared. Alpacas rarely spit. They are **prey** animals.

Alpacas are raised mostly as farm animals, but some people keep them as pets.

What's the Difference?

Both llamas and alpacas are herd animals. They look similar. They can even have babies together!

Llamas have long heads and ears. Alpacas have short heads and pointy ears. Llamas can spit and hiss. Alpacas are shy.

Llamas and alpacas can be raised together.

People use llamas as pack animals and for their wool. People use alpacas only for their wool. Both llamas and alpacas are useful farm animals.

LLAMAS

Coarse wool

Banana-shaped ears

Long faces

- Can weigh up to 250 pounds (110 kg)
- Can be used as pack animals or for wool
- Will hiss or spit at predators

ALPACAS

Pointy ears

Short faces

Soft wool

- Can weigh up to 200 pounds (90 kg)
- Only used for wool
- Will run away when scared

GLOSSARY

coarse (KORSS) Something coarse has a rough texture. Llama wool is coarse.

herd (HURD) A herd is a group of animals that live together. Many llamas live together in one herd.

livestock (LYV-stok) Livestock are animals that live on farms. Alpacas are a type of livestock.

mammal (MAM-ull) A mammal is an animal that has hair and gives birth to live young. Llamas are a type of mammal.

pack animals (PAK AN-ih-mulz) Pack animals are animals used to carry goods or belongings places. Llamas are sometimes used as pack animals.

predators (PREH-duh-tors) Predators are animals that eat other animals. Alpacas run away from predators.

prey (PRAY) Prey are animals that are eaten by other animals. Alpacas are prey for other animals.

wool (WOOL) Wool is a type of hair found on animals such as alpacas and llamas. Wool is used to make fabric.

TO LEARN MORE

IN THE LIBRARY

Buller, Laura. *Llamas*. New York, NY: DK Publishing, 2019.

Butterworth, Chris. *Where Did My Clothes Come From?* Somerville, MA: Candlewick Press, 2015.

Lindeen, Mary. *South America*. Mankato, MN: The Child's World, 2019.

ON THE WEB

Visit our website for links about llamas and alpacas:
childsworld.com/links

Note to Parents, Teachers, and Librarians: We routinely verify our Web links to make sure they are safe and active sites. So encourage your readers to check them out!

ACTIVITY

Draw a picture of a llama and alpaca. Your picture should clearly show the differences between the llama and the alpaca. Look at pages 20 and 21 for help.

INDEX